Achieve – An Ownership Mindset

Moving from W-2 employee to W-2 owner

Introduction:

We all play the sport of Life regardless of position or how well we play. Life is also like Physical Education class in school when growing up. You either want to play hard and play to win, play hard to simply enjoy the activity, or endure because it is required and end up standing in a huddle talking to a like-minded group of kids that just want to survive the hour and move on to math. You know what I'm talking about. Whether you "endured" P.E. class or loved it, do not simply endure life... This is a sport in which we all must play and participate. At what level will you choose to play? Will you excel in the sport, or become a spectator on the field of play – likely resulting in your getting run over by other players?

Regardless of what level at which you choose to play, our work life is a huge part of what category you fall into. There is no right or wrong category to fall into. It is simply important to understand what category in which you fall. Most people fall into some category of work life as an "employee worker". These folks go to work daily working for someone else and working towards someone else's work related goal. In reality,

98% of working individuals fall into this category. Another category can include those that work towards someone else's goals, but do so in order to also fulfill their personal work related goals. Last there are those that fall into the category of working towards fulfilling their personal and work related goals solely. We will go into more detail around these categories and help you explore what category in which you currently reside, and push you to determine whether you are living in the right category based on your personality and work related goals.

Many of us choose to leave the daily grind of 9 to 5 (or, more like 7:30 to 8:30pm) work life behind. If you are reading this, you are most likely one of us. Someone who is in the work life grind working towards someone else's work goals, but that wants to move into a self-employment mindset and life. Or perhaps you are someone that has already taken that leap and is where they need to be physically, but may need to understand better what a positive ownership mindset can do. Regardless of where you are within this spectrum, an ownership mindset will be key to your success or lack of success.

In the introductory book "Achieve", it was discussed that in order to reach true achievement, you must first designate an aspiration, then move towards learning as much as possible, practice what you have learned and create habits that eventually lead you to master what you initially aspired to. It was also discussed that this process leading up to achievement is never ending. It is so important to understand that, with an ownership mindset, you will never be satisfied with your achievements. This sounds daunting, however it is truly something to embrace. A top athlete that breaks a record early in their career doesn't hang it up and retire just because they broke the record and achieved a level of greatness. No, they aspire to break yet another record, win another championship, work towards Hall of Fame status. This takes consistent and habitual levels of learning, practicing, and mastering over and over again. This book will further explain what it takes to accomplish this. Mindset is everything... Anyone can aspire to do or be something, but it takes grit to move towards accomplishment. Grit takes an ownership mindset. Your overall mindset around work and life make all the difference. Dream, aspire, learn, do, practice, master consistently in life.

My primary work passion revolves around the real estate industry. Your passion might be real estate sales and service, it might be insurance sales and service, or perhaps your passion revolves around making something through manufacturing or educating others. It really does not matter where your passion lies, your mindset will either create a catalyst for success or failure. So, what does it take to create a mindset for success and achievement? What does it take to create an ownership mindset? If you work in a career that you love, but it just happens to be that you work for someone and towards someone else's goals, it is ok. There is nothing wrong with that. This book however is going to focus primarily on those that may be in that very position in their work life, but that want to make a huge change in their lives towards making a break into ownership and entrepreneurship. This will also apply heavily to those that are already in entrepreneurship mode and working for themselves and towards their own work-life goals.

Chapter 1: The Employee worker

All of us that get up in the morning, get ready for the day, and go do something that will earn money are participating in what we all call WORK. Work can suck or it can be one of the most rewarding aspects of life. You can work to accomplish someone else's goals, you can work towards someone else's goals and also meet your goals if those two opportunities align, or you can work solely towards your goals (the awesome byproduct of this is that you will most likely also be helping others to achieve their work-life goals). Regardless, that W-2 income that comes into your bank account magically every 1st and 15th can become as addicting as Crack. We become so habitually accustomed to it that it is difficult to see any other way. We as employee workers see it as a safety net, which is why when people get laid off or if there is any kind of disruption in that pay schedule for any reason, people FREAK OUT! They go through withdrawals as if they needed a hit. It is totally crazy. Think about taking total control of your life. Think about what it would be like to be in control of when and how much you pay yourself. Keep in mind, with that freedom also comes risk. It is those that are willing to take on a level of calculated risk that earn that freedom.

First, let's talk about working towards meeting someone else's goals. This is where 98% of working people live. 98% of workers live to work daily on behalf of someone else's dream and aspirations. Truthfully, there is absolutely nothing wrong with that, as long as working towards someone else's goals and dreams in turn allows you to accomplish yours – which may be totally non-work related. A job can be a meaningful means to an end. A way to simply accomplish money in order to fulfill a life situation that you enjoy. The most important thing to remember is while working as an employee, even if doing so simply to meet income goals that provide for you and your family, is that it is so important to ENJOY your work. Enjoyment in employee status work can come in several different forms. Much depends on you, your personality type, and whether you view work very logically or very emotionally. There is no right or wrong way in which to view working. Everyone is different in this way. There are really just two categories of employee workers. Think about it; do you get up daily and go to work looking forward to your time interacting with co-workers, engaging with clients, making decisions and guiding others to fulfill those decisions, or do you go to work daily solely looking forward to the 1st and 15th of the month because you are 100% motivated by a fat (or "Phat" if you're a

Millennial) paycheck? Most people fall into one of those categories or the other. Most employee workers do not overlap the two. Although many people do indeed fall into category one as an emotionally motivated worker and still love the paycheck due to its ability to allow them to fulfill on-going situations that accomplish an aspiration or dream unrelated to work or a job.

Most very conservative people will work for and towards other peoples work related goals. Although there is really no such thing as job security any longer, most of us that are at least 40 years old were trained to think that going to work for a company was the right thing to do, and really the only thing to do. I have seen that the generation behind mine of people under 40 years old seem to have a stronger risk tolerance regarding work and career.

My best friend growing up is a great example of someone that I would deem as a conservative decision maker. Gary was and is always someone that I admire, love to be around, and that I look up to. Looking up to him does not necessarily mean that I want to be like him, but it does mean that I admire him for who he is. Gary and I think very differently in many ways, yet we are like-minded in many ways as well. I think we can all relate to having friends and family that may describe a relationship in the same way. Gary, from an early age, has always been a pragmatic logical thinker. He stays within the lines of the law, social norms, and rules – as do I (for the most part). His father worked for the same company from start to finish. Gary too has worked for the same company from start to present day. For many, It is ingrained that this is the right and only logical path to an ultimate happy retirement. For Gary, it will be. He is an extremely successful and talented individual working in the Mechanical Engineering field for one of the largest companies in the world. I am sure he does very well and I know he is well liked and admired within his organization. Most professionals fall into Gary's work-life category. At one time, I too thought that my work path would fall in a similar trajectory. For over 17 years in my post collegiate work life it did. I worked for only two different organizations over my first 17 years of professional work life and worked hard to impress and build credibility within my field of work. I did so with much success. I was comfortable and made a good living in the banking industry. But for me, there was something missing. It was like a hole in my life that I simply couldn't put my finger on in terms of what that hole was. I was married, had a great home in a great neighborhood, had a beautiful daughter, a growing 401k, health insurance… What in the world is it that I was missing in my life? It was hard to figure out. It took me over a decade to realize what it was.

I realized, only after what I saw at the time as a tragedy, what it was that I was missing. And, I figured out that it wasn't that I was really missing anything in my life. Heck, I had everything I needed and more. What I figured out though was that for 17 years I had been swimming up stream against the current of my own inner mindset. Although Gary and I are a lot alike from an upbringing perspective and hold very similar positive personal and professional moral values, he and I are very different in our risk tolerance in regard to many things, including work life. I found only after getting fired from my last banking gig, that I was not meant to work for other people. I was meant to work for myself and towards my own work related and personal goals. I aspired to be accountable in my work life only to myself and to any people or coaches that I allowed into my life to hold me accountable. If someone other than me is in my life to hold me accountable, it is because I asked for them to. Not because I have to, but because I want to and know that we all need other people in our lives to hold us accountable to activities that work towards moving us beyond our comfort zones. Though Gary is pushed, challenged, and held accountable at a high level within his organization, that accountability is always being pushed down by someone higher-up that he reports to. Even CEOs of companies report to and are held accountable to a Board of Directors.

When I was fired from the bank at which I worked, I panicked. At the time I had been recently divorced and I was, or course, responsible for my daughter's safety, comfort, and overall well being financially and emotionally speaking. Having just lost my job, this was all in jeopardy in my mind. I scrambled to send out resume's to multiple other banks and started networking heavily to all of those I knew within other similar organizations. This reaction is only natural when this happens. Panic mode occurs, then reactive mode, then all the emotions that pour into you including self-doubt, worthlessness, fear of bankruptcy and financial ruin, etc... I began having paycheck withdrawals like a Crack addict. The crazy thing is that even as I was getting some interviews and even job offers from other banks, I still could not bring myself to feel better about my situation. I actually turned several jobs down. My primal instinct was to grab the first job that was offered, however something kept telling me not to settle. By this time, I had a lot of opportunity to reflect and think without the clutter of having a day to day job. This period of rest for me and my mind, though still very stressful due to the situation I was in, was so freeing and valuable. As I reflected back on my career, I realized that I really did not have a passion for what I was doing (and it probably ultimately showed – hence getting fired). I was one of those people in the category of working for the 1st and 15th each month. I was simply going through the motions within my work life. I was working for that high on the 1st and 15th. This realization and self-reflection caused me to really lean on the power of prayer. Every day and night I prayed for guidance and confidence in hopes God would lead me to make a decision that would set my life back on track. I know that many of you will find this really hokey or unbelievable, but I was inspired by something. I attribute this inspiration completely to God. He ultimately answered my prayers. I believe that God instilled in me, during one of the weakest moments in my life, the confidence, the will, the grit to actually pause and reflect on what it was that I really wanted to do and to be. He placed people and ideas in my life that make me who and what I am today. In reality He does this for all of us, if we open our hearts and our minds to Him. I let God into my life to do His work on me. The confidence of placing my heart in His hands led me to fill the hole that I had felt for decades. That hole for me was my not working for myself.

Once I realized that my passion around real estate, previously as a hobbyist investor, was really my true calling and my porthole to entrepreneurship and understanding that I could put my direction within God's hands, it freed me to get uncomfortable. It freed me to take some calculated risks around my next steps in life. I jumped into the first Real Estate licensing course I could find. I am licensed in North Carolina, and I did not realize this at the time, but the North Carolina licensure process for Real Estate Agents is one of the most stringent in the Nation. My ignorance around this fact helped me because I just dove in not having to worry about how "hard" it was to get licensed. Now, I will preface this by sharing with you that I was, at best, a mediocre student in school. I am a pretty smart guy, but from a school work and studying perspective, I was pretty slack and lazy. In school, I was likely to blow through my homework as quickly as possible so that I could get outside to play ball or ride my bike with buddies. To demonstrate, Gary and I both have last names that start with the first three letters "Har" so from Kindergarten all the way to our High School graduation, he and I were sat beside of each other. Anything that involved alphabetical order in school tended to throw us side by side. In 4th grade our Elementary School hired a new Principal, Mr. Kendrick. I could tell that Mr. Kendrick was a nice guy and easy to talk to. Within Mr. Kendricks first month on the job, one of his goals was to meet each and every student and know and understand something about each of us. So, it was no surprise when it was my turn to meet him, Mr. Kendrick, who had been efficiently calling us into his office in twos, Gary and I were both called to the office together to meet with him. I remember I sat down in front of his huge desk and Gary sat in the chair to my right. We could barely see over the top of the desk to see him. Mr. Kendrick proceeded to make some small talk and I recall that he asked both Gary and I one question. The question was: What are your two favorite subjects in school? Gary spoke up first and proceeded to explain that he really liked math and that his second favorite subject was Science. You can see that Gary's logical and practical nature began early in his life. Once Gary colorfully described the reasons he liked math and science best, Mr. Kendrick turned to me and asked me the same thing: Chip, what are your two favorite subjects? Having listened to the question carefully when Gary was asked, I had already determined in my mind the answers. So, with zero hesitation I looked at him and said, P.E. and Lunch... Yes, I told my new Principal that my two favorite subjects in school were play time and eating... Now, you can imagine Mr. Kendrick's reaction. I remember him leaning way back in his office chair with a grin on his face. I knew that our new Principal was an awesome dude when all he said back to me was: Well, that was the most honest answer I've heard all day. He continued to let me know that those were his two favorite subjects as well. To this day, I have run into Mr. Kendrick – long since retired - around town many times, and he still remembers that conversation and he always makes a point to remind me of how refreshing he thought the answer was. I share this story simply to demonstrate the difference between my personality and Gary's and to demonstrate my viewpoint of school. We are both good people. We are both successful in our own rights. Gary and I are, to this day, very close friends. However, he and I are different from one another and think differently. We are especially different in regard to risk tolerance when involving work and career decision making. We respect very highly those differences between us and I think it actually enhances our relationship. He does admit to me from time to time that he thinks I am crazy for heading in certain directions in life, particularly my work life, however I also think he finds it interesting. You can see that school and studying were not really my strong suit. I made fine grades, certainly enough to get by and to be able to get into College, but I was definitely not the straight -A- student that Gary was. Therefore, when my real estate class was over and it was time to take the class exam (passing the class exam is simply a prerequisite for being able to sit for the actual State and National level exams) I was seriously concerned about my likelihood of passing. I prayed more than I have ever prayed in my life leading up to that test. I took the class exam and waited about 30 minutes for my instructor to grade it nervously waiting to here the result. She finally called me in and simply said: You passed... I had passed by only one point, but I passed damnit. I remember thinking that there is no way in hell I actually passed that test. I completely attribute that passing grade to God. Then there was the official State and National examinations. This was a monitored proctored exam in a single cubical with a video camera watching you. Serious stuff. I remember sitting in that cold lifeless cubical and thinking, well it was a fun ride. I almost made it... I sat there for 3 hours and answered every single multiple-choice question. When I got up my butt was so numb I thought I was going to fall over. I limped my way out of the testing room and I remember seeing this lady walk over to a printer. She picked up a piece of paper and walked towards me. I thought I was going to puke I was so nervous. I think I was nervous about the grade, but I think I also felt some preemptive embarrassment thinking that I most likely failed miserably. She looked at me with a straight face and handed me the paper and said: You passed! I couldn't believe it. I had passed on my first try. I smiled and probably foolishly jumped up and down like a school girl and I remember I gave the lady a huge hug. I also remember that she did not smile back or reciprocate. I didn't care though... I was freaking on my way to selling real estate. I was on my way to entrepreneurship. In my mind, I was on my way to freedom. That was the beginning for me. My work life was about to change in a huge way. I knew that my work life would now always be different. I felt a little maverick. It was truly freeing.

Chapter 2: What's next?

I haven't been cured of the entrepreneurial bug yet. It has not been easy though. I do not think that anyone that has ever left the W-2 1st and 15th Crack addiction behind for uncertainty and an irregular pay structure thought it was easy. It is hard as hell. That is why the right mindset matters. For the remainder of this book, we will focus on entrepreneurship perspectives as it relates to the Real Estate industry. However, these principals can be applied and adapted easily to any sales business. Think about it, if you own a company, you are selling something to someone... It doesn't mater if you are in real estate sales, insurance sales, car sales, furniture sales, hospitality, or manufacturing. You are selling something to someone every day.

So, what's next? You have made the bold decision to pursue a life of freedom of choice and action. You have made the decision to take a risk and put the W-2 "employee" life behind you. First, it is important to reflect on why you are making this decision. Is it out of necessity or choice? Take time to reflect on what led you to this awesome, but scary decision. Were you laid off? Have you taken time away from work and now want to re-enter the working world? Did you simply hate your job? It really doesn't mater why you decided to move into a new work world, but it does matter that you first know and understand why. If it is to work fewer hours, to get rich quickly, or to stress less, then close this book and go back to your job. Understanding why is only the beginning of your mindset shift. The why question is answered. From there, determine next steps. I will assume that you are going into the real estate sales industry and that you have already taken steps to become licensed. I know that the licensure process is not an easy one in most states, so I offer you a HUGE CONGRATULATIONS!!!

Now that you are through school and you have your license to sell in hand, you may think the hard part is behind you. If you are like most newly licensed real estate Agents, you have spent the last 15 years watching House Hunters on HGTV and think that you can show a prospective buyer three different properties from which they will choose one within a 30 minute timeframe and that you will get paid major bank for doing very little. Reality check! This isn't a 30 minute episode of House Hunters. This is real life. Ask yourself a number of questions. First, on House Hunters, or in real life, how did the Agent acquire and meet the new prospects? Second, what did the rapport building process look like that eventually led to a sufficient level of trust? Third, how do you decide when it is time to put a client or prospect in your car to "haul and hope" that you show them the right property? To understand the right mindset of a business owner, and as a Real Estate Professional, you are a business owner, you have to learn, practice, and eventually master these things.

Learn as much as you can about your new trade. Attend training both inside and outside of the firm under which you choose to work. Partner up with one or two experienced seasoned veterans with the intention of apprenticing beside of them for several months. Hire a coach or productivity trainer for a period of time if necessary. It does not matter what methods you employee, it is simply important that you employee several opportunities to learn, grow, and practice what your business is all about. My company has a stellar coaching and training system that all new licensees enter. There are a number of small and large companies that offer similar opportunities. Plug into these training and accountability functions as often as possible in the beginning. As a Real Estate Professional, go into the business with the understanding that you do not know everything and that you are open to absorbing as much new information as possible from as many experienced people as possible. Read books! A great book that every Real Estate business person should read is Gary Keller's "Millionaire Real Estate Agent". It is the best business road map read I have encountered by far for business minded Real Estate Professionals. It is a must read and will guide you through the multiple activities that will lead you to overall success in building a massive real estate business. However, prior to absorbing and implementing a business plan as laid out in Keller's MREA, you must first get your mind right. You must first transition your mindset from one of an employee, to one of an owner. This is hard to do, but anyone can ultimately succeed.

So far, we have discussed the importance of learning and doing so from multiple different activities and people. One caution to you is this: Many new Real Estate Professionals fall into the trap of over-committing themselves to too much training. I have seen this happen over and over again to new licensees regardless of previous professional work experience. New Agents tend to go to training class after training class day after day because they lack confidence in what they know or don't think they know. They lack the confidence to just get out there and do the job. People in this situation may go to the office or attend webinar seminars and training modules on a full time basis for weeks and months. These folks may also feel like they are "working" hard and being really productive because they are learning and growing their knowledge of the industry. What they are missing though is the "practicing" aspect of learning. The NUMBER ONE best way to learn in any new business, is to simply do. Going to class all day everyday will may make you feel like you are being productive and may give you a reason to get out of bed in the morning, but too much of it can be VERY counter-productive. Do not fall into the trap of being over-prepared. What I mean by over-prepared is, you spend your days trying to get your files in order, because God knows you can't make a phone call to a prospect unless your files are in perfect order. Or, you may work on that perfect listing or buyer package for days constantly tweaking it to attempt perfection. Because God knows, you can't go on a listing presentation or meet with a new home buyer prospect until your folder of marketing paperwork is just right. Come on!!! Do not fall into this trap. Files are important. Listing presentations and buyer packets are important. Just know and understand that NONE OF THAT MATERS IF YOU DON'T HAVE A CLIENT. The FIRST thing you do is simply make contact with people in your life. Start with making contact either over the phone, text, email, or in person with everyone you know. You don't have to contact them to attempt to sell them something. You simply want to start out by making contact with people in your life to let them know what you are doing now. You have started a new business. Your business is Real Estate sales and consultation. Let them know that you would love their support in passing the word along. Ask for them to send you their business when the time comes, and to refer you to friends when real estate comes up in conversation. Everyone loves to talk real estate. Do not be afraid to talk to people in your life. This is the first step to "practicing" real estate. Dive into conversations. If asked questions you do not have the answer to, don't freak out. Just let them know that you would like to research that question a bit before answering and then follow up with them. These contacts are your next evolutionary step towards an ownership mindset. You took the risk to leave the 1st and 15th crack paycheck behind. You have invested in yourself and in your future. Now, why in Hell would you not take the "risk" of actually talking to a friend or acquaintance? That isn't a risk. It's a freaking conversation. Yes training and learning through others is important. It is the first step to success. However, don't use "training and preparation" as a crutch to avoid the activities that will actually bring you money. Training and preparing are a small part of a multipronged process that will lead you to success as a business owner. Talking to people, as many people as possible, on a daily basis about anything real estate related is doing it… Talking and making contact with as many people as possible to build or re-build relationships that may have waned over the years is doing it… Getting more involved at Church or within non-profit volunteer organizations where you interact and meet new people is doing it… This my friends is the art of practicing your craft. To use a Baseball analogy, increasing your number of "at bats" in any way is doing it… Your batting average can only increase if you actually have the opportunity to enter the game and step up to the plate to receive a pitch. So, as the famous Nike slogan says; "Just do it"!

I know that sports analogies and slogans are tired and overused, however I also know that very successful people excel in sport every single day. They excel in the sport of business. Yes, business is my sport! So, it is hard to step away from the analogies and slogans that some up my sport best. Just like an NFL player in an after-game interview, you may here phrases like:

"All of the daily practice and repetition paid off!"

"My team showed up and made it happen!"

"All of the practice and behind the scenes work really prepared us for this victory!"

"Coach had us study film, practice the game plan over and over again... "

"We were able to go out there and get the job done!"

These are all phrases I am able to use every day I go to work. I win! I win because I have developed the understanding of how important mindset can be. I understand what it takes to develop a winning ownership mindset. Just like a top athlete, it takes guts, endurance, failure, practice, repetition, more failure, and the right mindset to ultimately achieve success. You have made the decision to play in the sport of business. Now own it! Be accountable to it!

Chapter 3: The Sport of Business

Business is a sport. One of my mentor/coaches, Adam Hergenrother, introduced this phrase and philosophy to me. I love it. After hearing that phrase for the first time a couple of years ago, I adopted it and live by it. Top athletes, regardless of sport, identify themselves (from a professional perspective) by their sport. Others also identify them by their sport and their proficiency at performing at a high level. What makes you any different? Your sport is business. In relation to your professional identity, do you not want to be identified by those in your life, and by those not yet in your life (the public) as proficient in the performance of your sport? To become a top professional at anything, this is crucial. You have to take on the ownership mindset of a professional athlete. Don't get me wrong… This does not mean you have to lose 50 pounds, turn that keg of a gut back into a six pack, or become a Triathlete. It simply means you have to take on the mindset that learning, practicing, mastering, and living the sport on a daily basis is imperative.

When considering sport, the number one thing athletes of any kind attribute to their success is accountability. Accountability can come from many different places in your life and can take many shapes. Regardless of who you place in your life, or what systems you put in place to hold you accountable, this is such an important step. Without accountability to someone or something daily, you will fail. How do you hold yourself accountable? We are naturally accountable to our actions and activities in all we do each day. So, why not expand your overall level of accountability professionally? All top athletes have people and systems in their lives that hold them accountable to their daily activities and habits. Consider this and do the same. Hire a business coach, a productivity trainer/coach, partner with another professional as an accountability partner. Use your calendar as a system to hold you highly accountable. You would be surprised at the correlation between a well blocked calendar and a high level of achievement. Professionals who effectively time block every minute of their day using their calendar are factually more efficient, stress less, and experience a higher level of success and satisfaction of life. This is a fact. If you block time on your calendar daily for all activities, including meditation and/or exercise, alone time, family time, meals, and business related activities like meetings, appointments, email catch up time, and most importantly new client prospecting time, then you will never miss doing one of these activities. If it is on your calendar, it happens. If it is not on your calendar, it doesn't happen. Live by your calendar and you will fill a since of freedom that you have not felt before. It is a de-stressing item within your life that will pay dividends if you use it daily. This accountability will drive you consistently to do better, be more efficient, and produce more with less effort.

Accountability can also come in the form of leverage. What I mean by leverage is anything that you put into your life to assist you in making things easier and more efficient for you. This can be a system like a CRM (Client Relationship Management) tool, or it could be a person or people you put into your life to assist you, like a personal Assistant. Systems that make your life easier and create efficiencies for you and your clients are systems leverage tools. Your laptop is leverage, your mobile app is leverage, your e-signature software is leverage, your cell phone is leverage. You can see that anything and everything that makes your life a little more convenient is leverage. A very good Administrative Assistant can be a huge multiplying factor for you and your business from a leverage perspective. They can be worth their weight in gold. As your business grows, an Administrative Assistant should be one of your first hires. If they are good, they should add enough value for your business to double in volume within a year. That is how important leverage can be in your professional life. It may mean the difference between making $25,000 per year and making $1,000,000 in a year if employed and managed at a high level. Also, think of the byproduct accountability that hiring someone to work for you puts into your life. Now, you are responsible for you and your family, and for another person's livelihood and family. That is a major level of accountability. Do not be afraid of it! Embrace it! Own it!

Going back to the top athlete comparison, the factor that a high level of accountability naturally produces is the development of practice and habits. Practice, which leads to habit, is what comes of accountability. If you are held accountable by an effectively time blocked calendar, it is holding you to the activities that you entered into the calendar. If you are held accountable by a system CRM that flashes "to-dos" and follow-up reminders to you, it is holding you to be accountable for following up on those tasks and with those prospects. If you hire an Assistant and he or she is worth their salt, they are going to push you on a daily basis around goals and aspirations you described to them when you hired them. Your Assistant should manage you more than you manage them. A strong Assistant can be your guidepost every day as to what you have to do to make it a successful productive day. This can be intimidating, but man oh man can it help you multiply your earnings and ultimately your wealth. Conversely, if any form of leverage does not succeed in making your life easier, more productive, efficient, and move you towards higher earnings, fire it quickly. That includes any human leverage. I know that can be hard, but you need to get over it. Hire and implement slowly and fire quickly. Do not let any form of leverage drag you down. Most types of professional leverage cost money. That money can add up fast and pull you into an abyss of decline and failure. Hire slowly and be methodical in your search process. Make sure you hire the right people, and remember, if you discover they are not the "right one", fire them quickly. Don't waste time and drag it out. If an NFL Coach takes a team to a record of 2 wins and 30 losses over two seasons, the probability is they will be fired. If an NFL Coach hires an Offensive Coordinator after multiple seasons of 30+ points per game scoring, and the new season with the new Offensive Coordinator results in an average of 10 points per game, you can imagine that Coordinator position is going to be open again within a season. Hire slowly, fire quickly.

Chapter 4: "At Bats"

Earlier I told you that the number of "at bats" maters in the world of Baseball and any sales related business (and I hold the opinion that any and all businesses are sales related). If you are not at the plate with a bat in your hand, there is a zero percent chance you are going to get a hit. The same principal applies in your sport, the sport of business. From a real estate sales perspective, what do I mean by "at bats"? Well, simply put, "at bats" are the opportunities presented to you when you are in direct communication with another human being with a pulse. Anytime you interact with someone, that is an "at bat". It is what you do with that opportunity that maters most, but first and foremost you must step up to the plate as often as possible. Think of your business like a funnel. Many business related books, including Gary Keller's MREA book, describe what some refer to as the "business funnel, or "lead funnel", or transaction funnel". Think about it... A funnel has a wide mouth and a smaller skinnier base. If you place your business into a funnel shaped image it will look something like this:

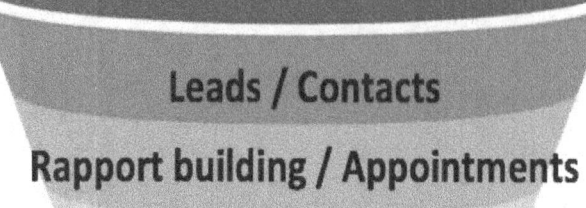

This is what I call the "Transaction Funnel". Look at it closely. You can see that the top (mouth) of the funnel is where your opportunities reside. This is where you are "at bat". In business you want for that funnel mouth to be as wide as possible. The size of your funnel mouth (number of at bats) has a direct correlation to the size of your funnel base (your closings $$$). This is why your number of "at bats" is so imperative. The real estate business in particular is all about getting you in front of as many people as possible on a consistent basis. From there, you participate through the additional levels of the funnel. It is in the meat of the funnel (middle area) where a deal is either won or lost. This is where your practice, positive business habits, and leverage take effect and either drive you to victory, or to failure. The "at bat" top portion of the funnel just gets you the opportunity to either succeed or fail.

The second layer of your Transaction Funnel is made up of Rapport building and appointment setting. Converting your leads (at-bats) into appointments happens here. Every step within the funnel is crucial to your success, but if you don't get the appointment, your "at bat" was wasted. You strike out! Lead conversion is an art, not a science. It doesn't take studying it, it takes practicing. It takes repetition; it takes failure; it takes disappointment; but from all of those experiences, you learn and you can ultimately master the art of conversion. To use the Baseball analogy again, lead conversion is the equivalent to getting a hit. In any type of business, people who perform at a high level have typically mastered the art of being able to build rapport quickly. Building a quick level of positive rapport with others is the first step to building an initial surface level of trust with someone. Rapport is crucial to getting the appointment. Rapport can be established in seconds over the phone. It doesn't take a long conversation or being in-person. Rapport in most cases, from a professional perspective, is establishing who you are, what company you are representing, and that you have the ability and tools to provide something that the person or prospect needs. - Hi, this is Chip with Harris Realty... Thank you for reaching out to me. I see that you have a question about the 123 Smith Street property.

I can help. What specific questions do you have regarding that property? - From there, shut up and let them talk. Let them talk about the house about which they initially inquired, but also prompt them to talk about themselves, their goals (as far as housing goes), about their kids, and about things that are important to them. Let them talk freely with you about anything important to them. Rapport building 100% takes getting the prospect to talk; it is not at all about you talking… Simply ask questions that are open ended and then ask for them to elaborate on their answers perhaps by saying, "tell me more"… People love to talk and they especially love to talk about themselves. It is human nature. Let nature take its course and let them talk. The instinct that you have to fight, is that same human nature instinct to want to talk about yourself. You must put your ego and your desire to talk about you, your family, your situation aside. Rapport is not built through talking, but through listening.

When you are successful at building even a surface level of rapport, you have set the table for getting the appointment secured. The key to remember here is, the primary reason many people fail at securing the appointment after working so hard to build rapport is, you **must ask** for the appointment. So many of us take the call or have a prospect finally pick up on the other end (so exciting), go through the process of quickly establishing credibility, share great rapport through asking awesome open ended questions, and then get soooo excited about such a productive call that we totally forget to ask for the appointment. Crazy huh? It happens all the time. It has happened to me, and it has (or will) happen to you. Ask for the business... Ask for the appointment. Day in and day out in business, your primary goal should always be to get appointments booked. Appointments lead to an opportunity for you to meet people in person which will allow you to then build additional credibility, trust, and ultimately a relationship.

As you can see in the image of the funnel, as you go through these steps, the opportunity to actually close on a deal and get paid gets smaller and smaller. That is why the mouth (at-bats) of the funnel needs constant growth and feeding. The funnel indicates that, from a business conversion standpoint, not every lead will call you back or reach out to you. Some leads just die. If a lead dies, there is zero opportunity to build rapport and set an appointment. Additionally, not all conversations with prospects (leads) that you do reach will turn into meaningful conversations and appointments. Then, even if you do get an appointment with a prospect, not all of those appointments will lead to a contract. Last, even if a contract is written, if you have been in the real estate business for any time at all, you know that a contract may not actually close. This is the primary reason I tell folks to interact with as many people as possible using all methods of communication because the more at bats you have, the more hits you will have, which will put you on base to eventually make it back to home plate for a score.

Trust building takes you to the next level within the Transaction Funnel. Credibility equals trust. When on your first appointment with a prospect, it is then that you want to take the opportunity to briefly share your professional qualities and attributes. This is your time to talk; but make it brief. They are not with you to hear all about your entire life. But when meeting for the first time, it is good, and expected, for you to add additional value to their goals by explaining how you will help them do so, and why that is important to you and to them. Establishing this brief but important position with your prospect will lend to your credibility and ability to assist them. This will create or expand trust. It takes trust to move anyone in your life from just a prospect, or just an acquaintance, to a relationship. This holds true in developing any relationship in life, personal or business. You know you have established a relationship when you ask for the business, and the prospect (now client) grants you their business. In North Carolina for me, this is when I ask the prospect to sign an Agency Agreement with me. That is the process of officially hiring me (my firm) to represent them throughout a transaction. Once they sign that agreement, they become a client. From there, the fun part begins and we complete the process of looking for the right property for them, finding it, negotiating an offer, getting inspections done, and then closing. As I said in the previous paragraph, there are a lot of potential pitfalls that lie between finding the perfect property, getting it under contract, and closing. You have financing to worry about and help to navigate, home inspections of all kinds that could blow up in your face, and then of course, personalities to manage and emotions to keep in check. This is not an easy gig! If you overlaid numbers over each category within the Transaction Funnel, in order to achieve a number 1 at the bottom of the funnel (equaling one closing), you would need to start with the number 100 at the mouth (top) of the funnel. That 100 would turn into 5 in the next category, which would turn into a 3 in the next, then a 2 which would ultimately create a singular closing (paycheck).

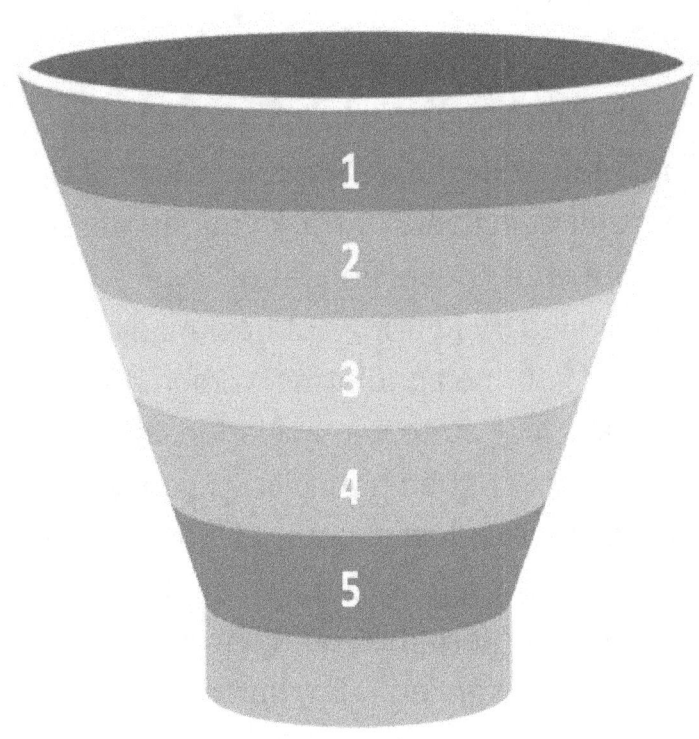

This diminishing funnel-like view is all about conversion. It takes 100 contacts to convert into 5 appointments, which lead to 3 relationships, which lead to 2 contracts, which leads to one closing. Conversion is key. Recognizing and understanding this philosophy is so important. It is important because if you understand the numbers, you will know how many contacts you need to make in order to close the number of deals you want or need to close to make the money you desire to make.

Chapter 5: Playing the Conversion Game

Converting a lead into a contact, then into a relationship, and ultimately a closing is where the practicing, failing, practicing more, failing more, and ultimately mastering comes into play. Knowing your numbers and being able to track your numbers will allow you to figure out your conversion ratio. Your conversion ratio is determined by figuring out how many contacts it takes for you to get one appointment, then how many appointments it takes for you to win a relationship (client – Agency Agreement in my case), then how many Agency Agreements it takes to make one closing occur. If you track all of the calls, attempted contacts, actual contacts, on down the line, you will easily be able to determine your conversion ratio. There will never be an ideal conversion ratio, but you can research and determine industry averages. But, you are not an average person if you are reading this book. So, what does it take to become "above average" or a master at conversion? It takes a ton of practice. In this case practice means at bats. It always comes back to your number of at bats. It always boils down to opportunities or lack of opportunities. Remember, at bats are opportunities. How many at bats does it take for you to get a hit, or better – a home run? As you work through this "at bat" model on a consistent level, the better you will become at perfecting your conversation scripts, the better you will become at transitioning a conversation into an appointment, an appointment into a client, a client into a closing... Just like a top athlete trains hard to earn playing time, we must train hard to convert leads into closings. The athlete wants as much playing time as possible because he or she knows that time on the court or on the field is invaluable to their success. If they are not in the game, the can not shine they can not fail and learn, they can not get better as quickly. Practice is so important in any sport; why should our sport be any different? Conversion is all about practicing which will lead to both successes and failures, both from which you can learn and make improvements.

Your conversion rate can make a huge difference to your bank account. Think about it... If you have a low conversion rate, it might take your making 300 contacts to result in one closing. Yet, if you practice your trade and master the art of conversion, you could drive that number down to 50 contacts resulting in a closing, or 25 contacts into a closing... Whatever the number, improving the conversion process can really create a compounding effect on your earnings and net worth. Say for example you have a listing that is priced at $580,000. Let's say your firm's commission rate is 3% as a standard. You can see that closing that property will gross your firm 3% of $580,000 which equals $17,400. Someone that converts 300 contacts into one closing makes $17,400. But, if someone can master conversion to the point that they turn one closing every 50 contacts, they would earn $104,400 versus just $17,400. You see? The proficient Agent is going to make the same 300 contacts that the less proficient Agent makes, yet their 300 contacts turns into six closings (one for every 50 contacts) versus one closing for the less proficient Agent. Practicing and mastering your trade is so crucial. I hope the example above demonstrates just that.

Make your lead conversion ratio into a game. Track the numbers and statistics just as a Baseball analyst tracks player stats. Your "player stats" will reveal opportunities to improve and will paint a perfect picture of your strengths. Make it a game to improve your stats. Challenge yourself, or better yet, make sure your accountability partner or coach knows your stats and knows what you are striving to accomplish. They will push you to be your best and to practice, create habits, and maintain a strong level of commitment to yourself and your dreams.

Chapter 6: Living the Business

Those who can ultimately achieve an ownership mindset have figured out that, to do so, you must learn how to live the business. What do I mean by "live your business"? I take it back to the understanding that the top athlete has in regard to how they are identified. Tom Brady is identified by most as one of the greatest Quarterbacks to ever play the game. Magic Johnson is identified as a Champion, MVP level, and Hall of Fame basketball player. Jack Nicholas is identified as one of the most proficient golf professionals ever. How will you be identified professionally? To really own your business, you have to be identified professionally out in the public as an expert in your field. This can be accomplished in many different ways, and all ways are just as important as the other. Marketing, Branding, Community Involvement, wearing your brand on your shirt or jacket (literally), wearing a name bag, even when grocery shopping, becoming present on Social Media in a larger way. All of these categories are important. It costs very little money to invest in a name tag or some logo clad clothing. It costs virtually nothing to create a brand for yourself that you can use as an easily identifiable logo, company name, and company tag line (a short description of what makes you different). That brand can be marketed via social media for free and via print very inexpensively. No mater what you create for yourself, or have a branding and marketing expert create for you, it is important to tout it proudly and often wherever you go. Playing golf with the fellas on Saturday. Wear your company's golf shirt versus a non-branded shirt. Going out to eat for lunch, don't forget to put your name tag on your shirt or jacket. Live the business. Become identifiable.

When you live your business, you must realize that you are always "on". This is a huge differentiating factor when compared to being an "employee worker". A business owner has to be good with never turning "it" off. Now, this doesn't mean you never unplug, or rest. I live my business every single day, however, I never interrupt time with my kids or wife if that time is blocked on my calendar. However, they know that if we are out together or in a social situation with people we know or with strangers, I am always willing to engage in a conversation about Real Estate. It is expected. As a mater of fact, if I am out with friends or at social functions and conversations around Real Estate do not happen, I have failed. I have wasted many at-bats. People love to talk Real Estate, so always being "on" means you need to always be prepared to have conversations regarding the subject. Practice giving creative answers to the "typical" questions… "How's the market?" "How are things selling?" "You staying busy?" Be ready with creative answers to these questions because if you are doing your job and living your business, people will know what you do for a living and they will identify you as an expert in the field. This will draw them to you and to ask these questions, even if they are just asking to make small talk. Small talk can result in a referral or an opportunity. You never know. Become a business rainmaker for yourself and for your business. Make it rain business... The only way to do that is to perfect getting as many at-bats as possible and by living your business in the community. This fact holds true to any entrepreneur business owner. It doesn't matter if you sell Real Estate like me and my company, or if you manufacture widgets. It is vital that you live it, day in and day out...

Your business is like a baby being born into your family. It takes a village to raise that baby into a questioning, learning toddler, then into an independent teen, and ultimately into a respected well raised young adult. If you treat your business as a child, you will see it takes a lot of time, care, nurturing, love, discipline, laughter, tears, successes, and failures... But, you will also see a healthy progression in how you handle the business. In the baby stage, much like with a new-born child, you are expected to have a lot of long days, sleepless nights, and to give constant attention feeding and changing the baby. In the beginning you will experience the same with your business. Much like a child though, eventually the baby (business) grows, begins to expand both physically and in maturation, and sprouts into a teenager in the blink of an eye. When your business matures in this way, your role changes. Over time, you will go from a one person show doing everything for everyone, to someone who hires people to do everything for everyone, to someone who watches people hire people to do everything for everyone. Your child in life eventually becomes less and less dependent on you. You are never out of their life, but when they grow up and become an adult, you gain freedom in choosing when and how to assist them, versus being the only one that can assist them and being expected to do so as a good parent. Your business too will sprout, grow, mature, and eventually need you in different ways. A high attention to leverage in your life will move you towards that "mature business" a lot faster. Putting systems and people into your life to drive your goals home is the way to go. But, it first takes that healthy, but not easy, nurturing process and many successes and failures over the years to master hiring the right systems and people into your life. Think of the possibilities though… The sky is the limit! There is no glass ceiling on entrepreneurship. There is no lack of opportunity. As you drive down the road, notice "For Sale" signs in peoples yards. Are they your "For Sale" signs, or someone else? If they aren't yours, you lost an opportunity. You most likely lost the opportunity because you were never "at-bat" with those prospective clients. Someone else was there in the right place at the right time. They may have been living their business… I will tell you this: When I see other Real Estate Agent's signs in people's yard, it pisses me off! I am not pissed at the home owner, or at the other Real Estate professional… I am pissed at myself and the people I have partnered with within my organization. Where was I? Where the hell were we when this opportunity presented itself? We should have been there… I should have been there. People say there is room for more Real Estate Agents... That there is plenty of business to go around. Well screw that! I (we) should have that business. If other Agents want to gain that business, they need to understand they are only going to acquire it if they work for or partner with me. I know that seems direct and maybe even a little untactful, however, that is living your damn business. Take great joy in your successes and learn from and improve upon your mistakes. The buck stops with you! No excuses - Live your business!

Chapter 7: Perception is Everything – Are you a Lion or a Rabbit?

I do not know how many times I have heard the phrase "fake it till you make it" in this business. I hear it all the time from real estate coaches, team leaders, firm owners, peers... I used to use that phrase a lot as well when teaching classes to newer Agents. Fake it till you make it! What does that phrase mean to you? Initially for me, I used it to encourage Agents to be confident outwardly even if intimidated or nervous internally. Seems like a pretty positive message on the surface, however as my career matured and I began to think of being more strategic in my thinking and in my teaching, I began to really dislike that phrase. Think about what it says: Fake it till you make it... You are asking someone to fake that they actually have knowledge, fake that they actually have consultative skills, fake that they can move a client through a transaction seamlessly. I do not think faking anything is positive. Now, I hate that phrase. When I hear it I kind of pucker up. Let's think about this differently... My encouragement to you through the remainder of this chapter and book will center around creating a positive perception. We will no longer discuss "faking it" in any way.

In this business, perception really is everything. Think about it, in life perception is everything. We all have to admit that perception is reality. What people think they see and hear from us creates their real thoughts of us and about us. Perception is reality! If perception is everything, then it is really important to understand how you want for people to perceive you. Your control over how people feel about you or how they think about you is called branding. We all brand ourselves personally and professionally constantly. Whether we like it or not, it matters what other people think about us. If perception matters that much, don't you think the "live your business" moto walks hand in hand with creating a perception or brand that which you want to be identified? You bet!

If perception is everything and perception forms reality in regard to how people view us, then I hope you can see that confidence, or at least the perception of a high level of confidence is key. As a new licensee, or an Agent that has not yet found their footing, it can be a daunting task to get out there and do what you need to do. And we all know what you need to do is step up to bat as many times as possible. You can't get a hit unless you step up to the plate. So, how do you develop confidence over night? Confidence is only developed by doing the job... By failing, learning, and doing it more. But what if you haven't gained that experience? What if your first opportunity, or at-bat, just happened? This is where you have to create and control people's perception of you. Take and own control of your brand. This takes being confident in yourself as a human being and as a Real Estate professional. You are a professional. You took that hard ass class and passed it... You paid your dues, literally, and obtained your Realtor status. You are a Pro! Act and think like one! What is your fear? Most say their biggest fear is either being rejected or embarrassing themselves by not having answers. Folks, this isn't rocket science. Go through all of the steps we discussed earlier in this book around building rapport, establishing trust, developing a relationship, etc... All it takes is being a person who knows how to make conversation. The main thing to remember is, you do not know everything and you will never know every answer to every question. Give yourself a pass and permission to always default to the phrase: "Let me get back with you on that". "Let me look into that for you". "I would love to research that a little more". "Can I follow up with you on that?" It is ok and totally expected and respected by people for you to have to follow up with them with answers. As a matter of fact, doing this, versus telling them something that you hope is correct, actually creates a higher level of credibility than shooting off an answer quickly. Let them know you are working hard for them. Part of that is discovering things pertinent to their needs on their behalf and following up. They need you as leverage in their life just as much as you need systems and people as leverage in your life. You are needed, you have the license to sell, you have all the knowledge you need to take the first steps through the Transaction Funnel. Just be confident in yourself and in your ability to get answers for people. You have people around you in your professional life that will help answer questions and lead you in the right direction. If all else fails, there is always Google to turn to (for some things). All of this equates back to leverage. Set yourself up for success by putting those leverage tools in place early.

Remember, regardless of how you play in the sport of life, just make sure you chose to play. Don't be a spectator. Make sure you learn and understand your strengths. Are you a life-long "employee-worker" where you a content working for someone else and towards someone else professional goals and objectives? If so, that is fine. Again, that is where 98% of people live. But, if you are one of the two percenters that feel a void within the "employee-worker" world and can't figure out what it is, take some time to really reflect on what drives you. You may have the entrepreneurial bug! Don't resist it! Research your passions and determine if there is a path to business ownership around that passion. I love Real Estate and I knew that there was a viable path to ownership and ultimate freedom around that field of business. If Real Estate is it for you as well, which I hope it is, then get through the class and exam as quickly as possible and plug into a well equipped firm or Real Estate Team right away. Begin the learning process by talking to and mentoring under one or more seasoned Agents. Hire a productivity coach, or at a minimum hook up with a group of other new licensees to form an accountability group. Whatever you do, just learn as much as you can as quickly as you can. That learning phase will be a little heavy in the beginning, but keep in mind that you DO NOT want to make "training and preparing" your daily job. Do not fall into the perpetual training cycle and don't fall into the lull of thinking you are being ultra productive just because you got up in the morning and went to, yet another, training class. Take stock in learning, but get out there and practice. Practicing and failing is also learning. Failing is actually the BEST way to learn. We call it failing forward. As a business owner, you will constantly endure failure. It is what you do with that failure and what you learned from it that matters. Fail forward often! It is uncomfortable at first, but over time you will learn to embrace it. You will seek it out. If you never fail, it means that you are not taking enough risk. You are not reaching and stretching yourself, your company, or your co-workers if you are not failing in a forward direction. Practice, do, practice do, fail, then practice and do again. That is what it takes. That is grit! An ownership mindset takes a lot of grit. Grit comes with endurance. You can be really enthusiastic, but endurance is what will make it happen for you. Endurance will create a solid business. Endurance will create wealth for you. To develop an ownership mindset, you must understand that it isn't a cake walk. Your grit and endurance will see you though. It will take endurance to create a huge mouth to your Transaction Funnel. You need a ton of at-bats in order to create the funnel you want and need for your business. The wider the mouth, the bigger the bottom will be. Expand yourself and stretch yourself to be in front of as many people as possible. This will increase your at-bats and ultimately your batting average (conversion rate). In order to do that, you must always want to enter the game. You must always be willing to step up to the plate. You must always be willing to swing and miss... Again, do not be afraid of failure. Failure will help you develop and strengthen your grit, endurance, and ultimately your bottom line. Getting in front of as many people (prospects) as possible takes living your business. Living your business does not mean working 24/7. Actually, it means the opposite. It simply means that you are being purposeful around creating a brand for yourself as a professional in your field of business. A "Pro" in your sport... The sport of business. Be in control of how people perceive you. Perception is key. Make sure you achieve the perception you desire. A perception of confidence can be just as effective as actual confidence, as long as you follow it up with results. Are you a lion or a timid rabbit? The answer doesn't matter as long as you give off the perception of a lion. No one can develop trust and credibility with prospects as a timid rabbit.

Let them see you as a lion. No fear... Confidence is in the eye of the beholder. The longer you are in business, the more you learn, practice, fail, practice more, then master your trade, the more confidence you will create for yourself. Until that occurs, make sure people at least perceive you as confident. Live your business and stay in control of your perceived brand on a constant basis. Living your business is not working 24/7, so ensure that you don't. If you do, you will burn-out. Create disciplines around your schedule. The best way to do this is by using a calendar (system) at a high level and by ensuring you are blocking every minute of your day on the calendar (even alone time, friend time, family time, exercise time, etc,,,). Block it all! Make it a game. If it isn't on your calendar, it doesn't exist. This kind of discipline will be so freeing to you. People want to work for themselves to create freedom and flexibility. Yet, most business owners work longer hours by far than they did when in the "employee-worker" category. I do believe business owners work harder in general than employee-workers, because they are nurturing a childlike business. We know and understand that we solely are responsible for raising that childlike business, for praising it, disciplining it, and pushing it beyond it's comfort zone until it matures. We set the standards and rules. We enforce boundaries and disciplines... But remember, it takes a village. Just always lean on your systems and on key people in your life as leverage. Leverage, including your calendar, is what will free you... But, in order for it to happen you have to become very disciplined around using leverage effectively. Using leverage through systems and people effectively will accelerate your businesses maturity tenfold. The right leverage creates a compounding effect just like compounding interest within a bank account. It will multiply on itself over and over again. If it doesn't, then fire it quickly and go out and find the right fit. Hire and implement slowly, but fire quickly. Nurture and raise your business to maturity just as if it were your child. Live your business every day! Within you, this will develop and Achieve, An Ownership Mindset.

ACHIEVE – An Ownership Mindset!

www.ingramcontent.com/pod-product-compliance
Lightning Source LLC
Chambersburg PA
CBHW071150220526
45468CB00003B/1010